DISCOVER!

CALLING ALL COMMUNITY HEROES!

WHO SAVES ANIMALS IN DANGER?

BY THERESA EMMINIZER

Enslow PUBLISHING

Please visit our website, www.enslow.com.
For a free color catalog of all our high-quality books, call toll free 1-800-398-2504 or fax 1-877-980-4454.

Cataloging-in-Publication Data
Names: Emminizer, Theresa.
Title: Who saves animals in danger? / Theresa Emminizer.
Description: Buffalo, NY : Enslow Publishing, 2025. | Series: Calling all community heroes! | Includes glossary and index.
Identifiers: ISBN 9781978542242 (pbk.) | ISBN 9781978542259 (library bound) | ISBN 9781978542266 (ebook)
Subjects: LCSH: Animal welfare–Juvenile literature. | Animal rescue–Juvenile literature. | Animal shelters–Juvenile literature.
Classification: LCC HV4708 .E495 2025 | DDC 179'.3–dc23

Published in 2025 by
Enslow Publishing
2544 Clinton Street
Buffalo, NY 14224

Designer: Tanya Dellaccio Keeney
Editor: Theresa Emminizer

Photo credits: Cover (background) ASTA DESIGN/Shutterstock.com; cover (speech bubble) mejorana/Shutterstock.com; cover (dog) JaimePorElMundo/Shutterstock.com; cover (person and cat) VGstockstudio/Shutterstock.com; p. 5 ANURAK PONGPATIMET/Shutterstock.com; p. 7 AP Images for The HSUS/AP Images; p. 9 Martin Mecnarowski/Shutterstock.com; p. 11 ORION PRODUCTION/Shutterstock.com; p. 13 Refluence/Shutterstock.com; p. 15 J.Kozak/Shutterstock.com; p. 17 BearFotos/Shutterstock.com; p. 19 LightField Studios/Shutterstock.com; p. 21 Aaaarianne/Shutterstock.com.

Printed in the United States of America

CPSIA compliance information: Batch #CWENS25: For further information contact Enslow Publishing, at 1-800-398-2504.

CONTENTS

BOLDFACE WORDS APPEAR IN WORDS TO KNOW.

FURRY FRIENDS

Whether they're sweet dogs, caring cats, or soft bunnies to hold and pet, animals are furry friends that fill our hearts with joy! But sometimes animals get into trouble. Who saves animals when they're in danger? Community heroes do!

ANIMALS CAN BE DEAR FRIENDS AND SPECIAL PARTS OF OUR FAMILIES.

THE HUMANE SOCIETY

The Humane Society of the United States is a national organization, or group. It rescues, or saves, animals and fights against the mistreatment of animals. It takes care of animals in **emergencies**. There are also many **local** humane society groups.

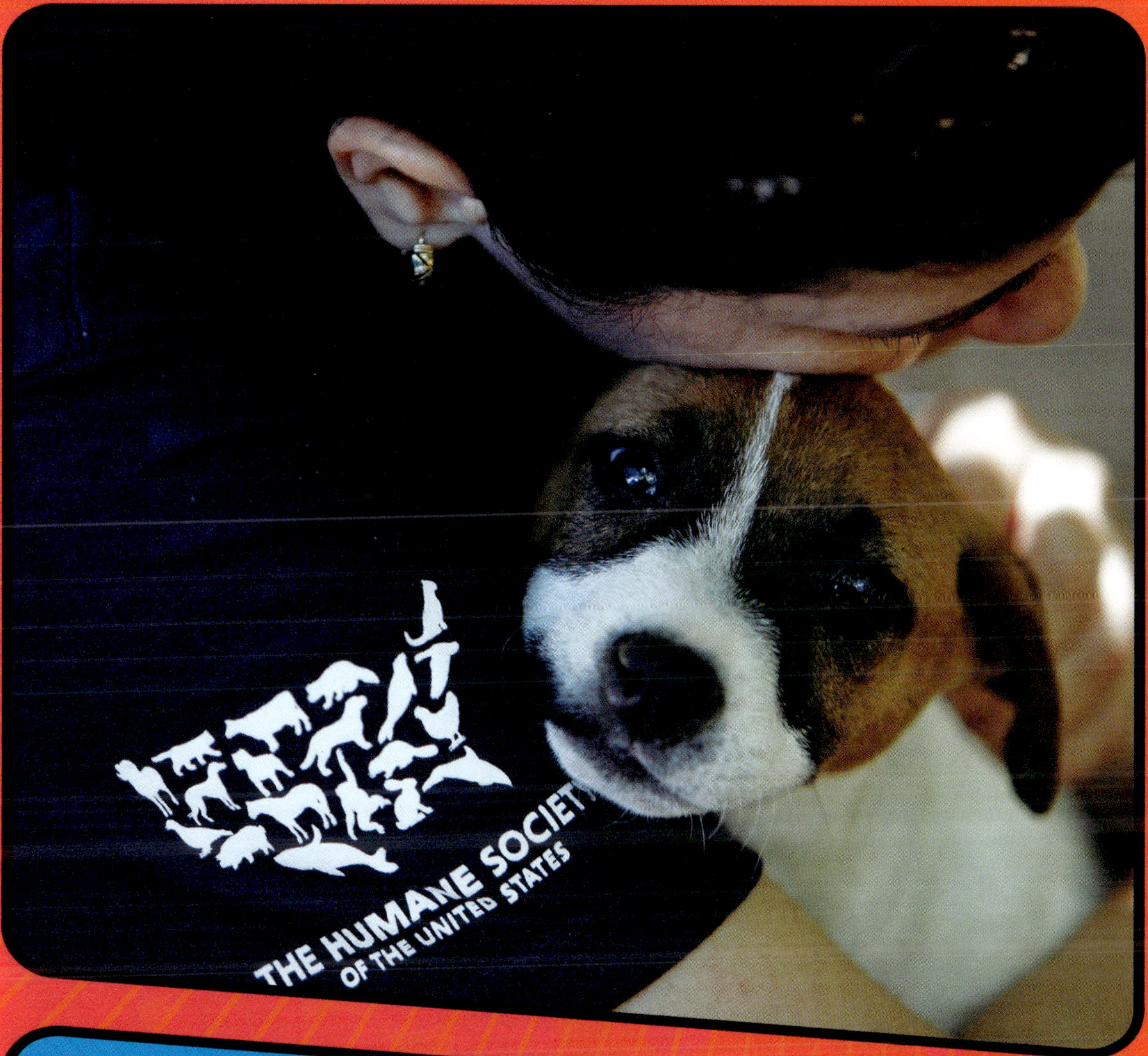

MEMBERS OF A HUMANE SOCIETY WORK TO END PRACTICES THAT HARM ANIMALS.

ANIMAL RESCUE TEAMS

Animal rescue teams are made up of specially trained people who save animals in danger. When a **natural disaster** happens, animal rescue teams make plans to move animals away from harm. They also make sure animals have the food, water, and care they need.

WILD ANIMALS ARE PUT IN DANGER BY DEADLY NATURAL DISASTERS, SUCH AS WILDFIRES.

VETERINARIANS

Veterinarians are animal doctors. They treat injured, or hurt, animals. They also give animals the **vaccines** they need to stay healthy. Some veterinarians work in mobile units, which are trucks or vans that can be driven to different places.

VETERINARIANS ARE A KEY PART OF ANIMAL RESCUE MISSIONS.

POLICE

Police can step in to stop people from mistreating animals. Sometimes owners neglect animals, meaning they don't take care of them properly. Others abuse, or hurt, animals. Although it's against the law, dogfighting is a big problem in the United States too.

POLICE CAN HELP STOP ANIMAL ABUSE.

FIREFIGHTERS

Firefighters are also community heroes that save animals! Although a firefighter's first objective is to help people in need, firefighters often save pets and farm animals from fires too. Firefighters also help **evacuate** animals from dangerous situations. Some fire stations help lost pets too.

THESE FIREFIGHTERS ARE HELPING A HORSE THAT FELL INTO A PIT.

ANIMAL SHELTERS

Animal shelters are a safe place for animals to stay when they're hurt, lost, or need a home. Many of the community heroes who work at animal shelters are **volunteers**. They care for animals and help them find homes.

YOU DON'T HAVE TO BE A PROFESSIONAL TO HELP ANIMALS. KIND, CARING PEOPLE CHANGE ANIMALS' LIVES!

MANY HELPERS

Animal rescue teams, veterinarians, police officers, firefighters, and shelter workers all save animals in danger. The kind of training needed to do these jobs differs greatly. However, having hands-on experience, or the skills and knowledge gained by doing something, is key to all.

EARNING A VETERINARY DEGREE USUALLY TAKES ABOUT EIGHT YEARS.

DO YOUR PART

You can help keep animals safe too! Here are some ideas to get you started:

- Take good care of your pets
- Gather supplies for your local animal shelter
- Learn more about animals and share what you know!

YOU CAN MAKE A DIFFERENCE! WITH HELP FROM AN ADULT, YOU COULD RAISE MONEY FOR A HUMANE SOCIETY OR EVEN ADOPT AN ANIMAL!

WORDS TO KNOW

degree: An official paper given to someone who has completed certain classes at a college or university.

emergency: An unexpected situation that needs quick action.

evacuate: To withdraw from a place for protection.

local: Having to do with a particular area, such as a city or town.

mission: A task or job a group must perform.

natural disaster: A sudden and often terrible event that happens in nature, such as a major storm or flood, that causes a lot of damage and even deaths.

professional: Someone who does a job for a living.

vaccine: A shot that keeps a person or animal from getting a certain sickness.

volunteer: A person who works without being paid.

FOR MORE INFORMATION

BOOKS

Pidcock-Reed, Heather. *Rescue & Adoption.* Philadelphia, PA: Mason Crest Publishing, 2022.

Romero, Libby. *Animal Doctors*. Washington, DC: National Geographic Kids, 2023.

WEBSITES

ASPCA
www.aspca.org/get-involved
Find out more about how you can help animals in need.

National Geographic Kids
kids.nationalgeographic.com/videos/topic/mission-animal-rescue
Learn more about the challenges that wild animals face and what can be done to help them.

Publisher's note to educators and parents: Our editors have carefully reviewed these websites to ensure that they are suitable for students. Many websites change frequently, however, and we cannot guarantee that a site's future contents will continue to meet our high standards of quality and educational value. Be advised that students should be closely supervised whenever they access the internet.

INDEX